CW01163129

# OUTBREAK!

# EBOLA OUTBREAK

KENNY ABDO

Fly!
An Imprint of Abdo Zoom
abdobooks.com

## abdobooks.com

Published by Abdo Zoom, a division of ABDO, P.O. Box 398166, Minneapolis, Minnesota 55439. Copyright © 2021 by Abdo Consulting Group, Inc. International copyrights reserved in all countries. No part of this book may be reproduced in any form without written permission from the publisher. Fly!™ is a trademark and logo of Abdo Zoom.

Printed in the United States of America, North Mankato, Minnesota.
102020
012021

**THIS BOOK CONTAINS RECYCLED MATERIALS**

Photo Credits: Animals Animals, AP Images, iStock, Science Source, Shutterstock
Production Contributors: Kenny Abdo, Jennie Forsberg, Grace Hansen
Design Contributors: Dorothy Toth, Neil Klinepier, Laura Graphenteen

**Library of Congress Control Number: 2020910906**

**Publisher's Cataloging-in-Publication Data**

Names: Abdo, Kenny, author.
Title: Ebola outbreak / by Kenny Abdo
Description: Minneapolis, Minnesota : Abdo Zoom, 2021 | Series: Outbreak! | Includes online resources and index.
Identifiers: ISBN 9781098223281 (lib. bdg.) | ISBN 9781098223984 (ebook) | ISBN 9781098224332 (Read-to-Me ebook)
Subjects: LCSH: Ebola virus disease--Juvenile literature. | Hemorrhagic fever--Juvenile literature. | Epidemics--Juvenile literature. | Epidemics--History--Juvenile literature. | Plague--History--Juvenile literature.
Classification: DDC 614.49--dc23

# TABLE OF CONTENTS

Ebola .......................... 4

Symptoms...................... 8

Source ........................ 10

Outbreak! ..................... 14

Glossary ...................... 22

Online Resources .............. 23

Index ......................... 24

# EBOLA

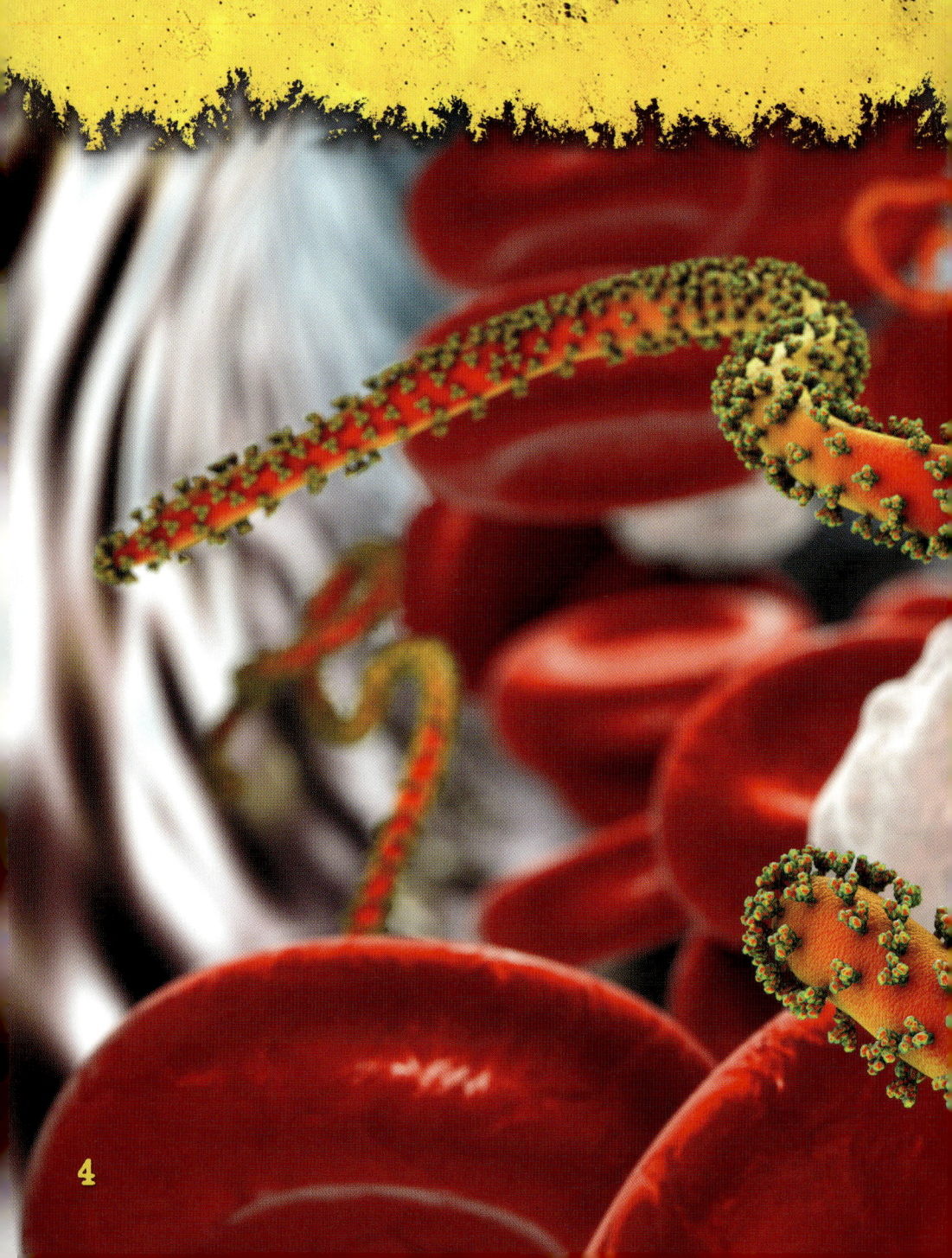

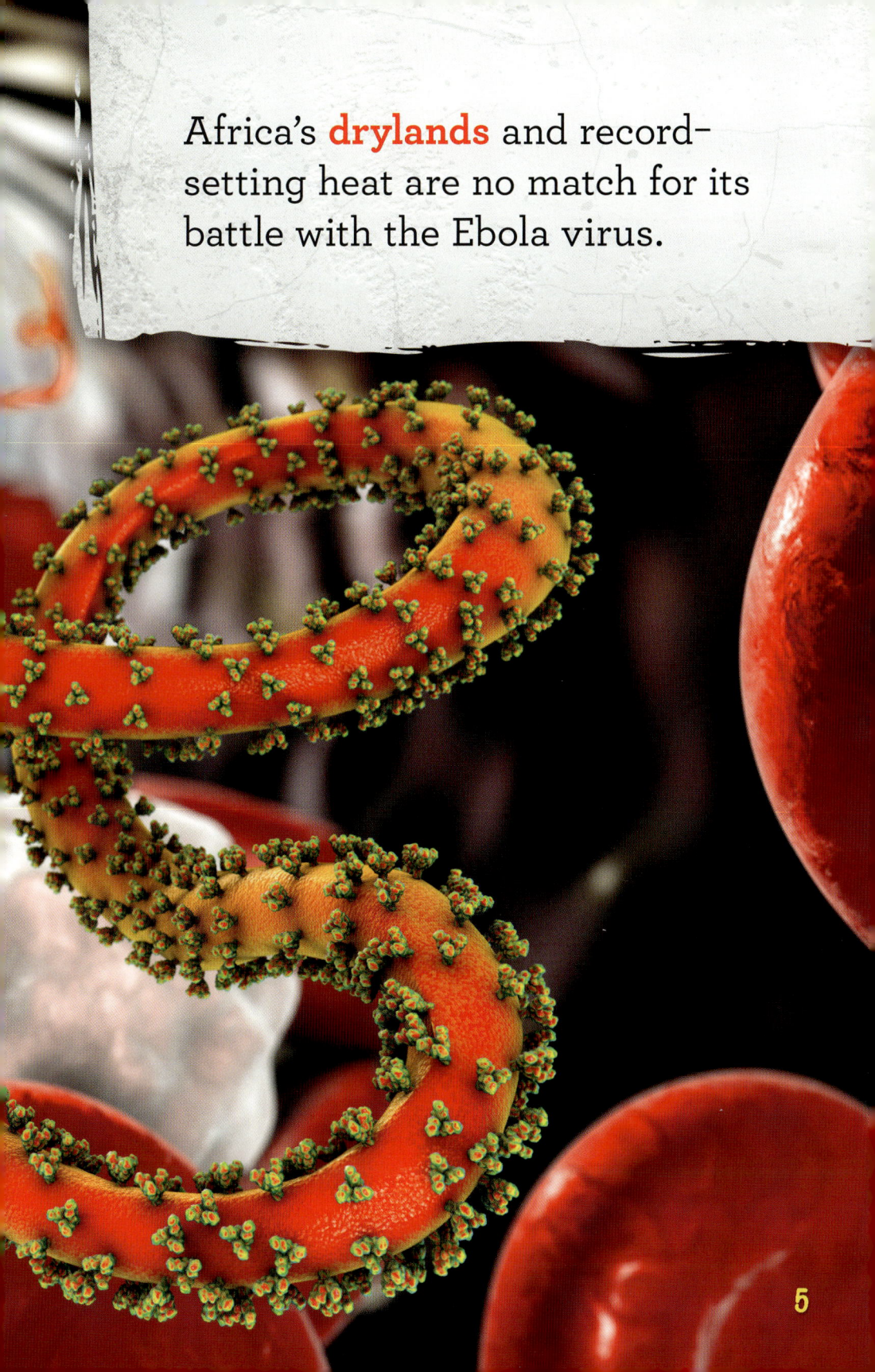

Africa's **drylands** and record-setting heat are no match for its battle with the Ebola virus.

6

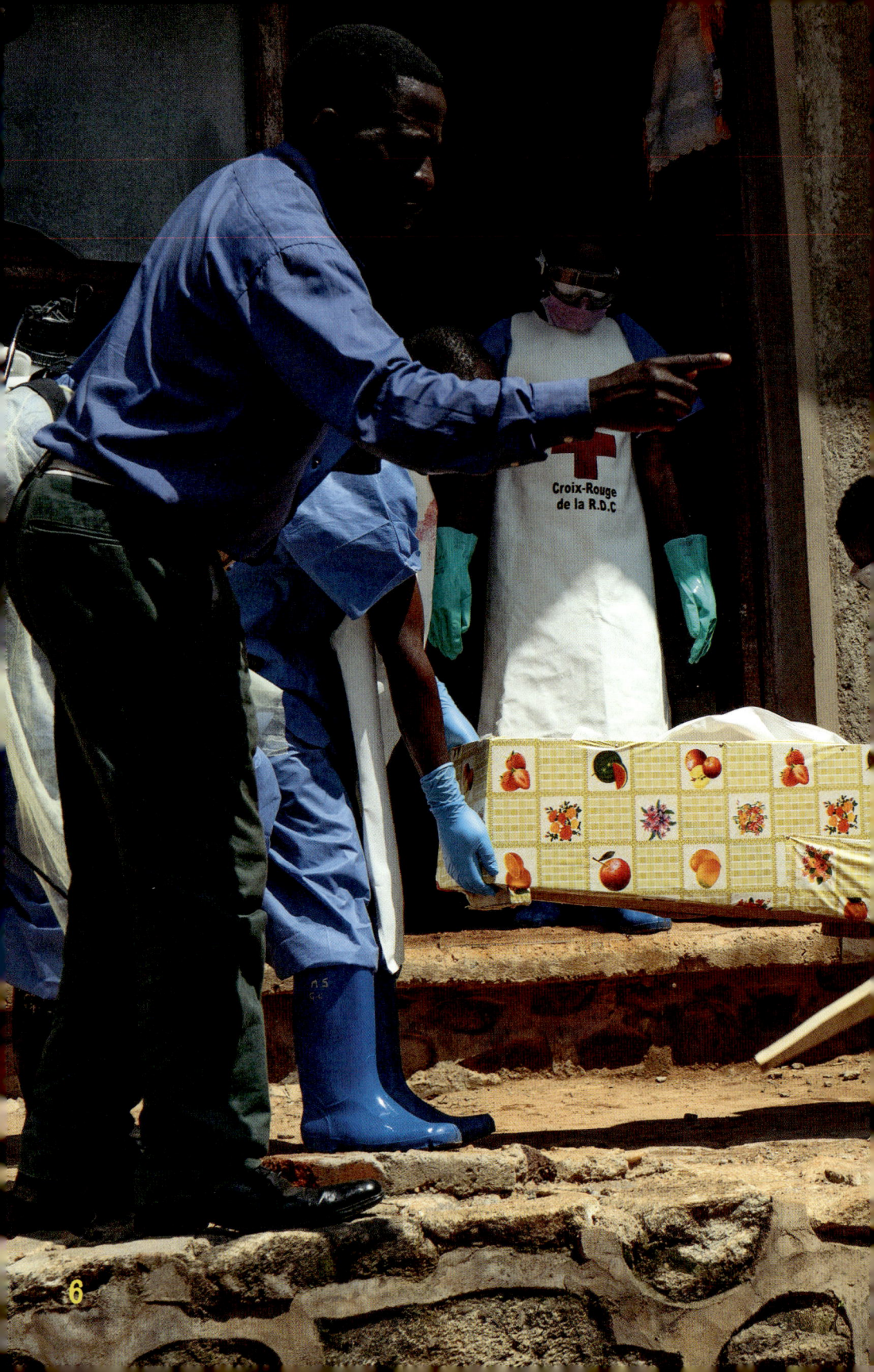

The infectious disease has run wild throughout the continent for decades.

# SYMPTOMS

Ebola **symptoms** include fever, aches, and vomiting.

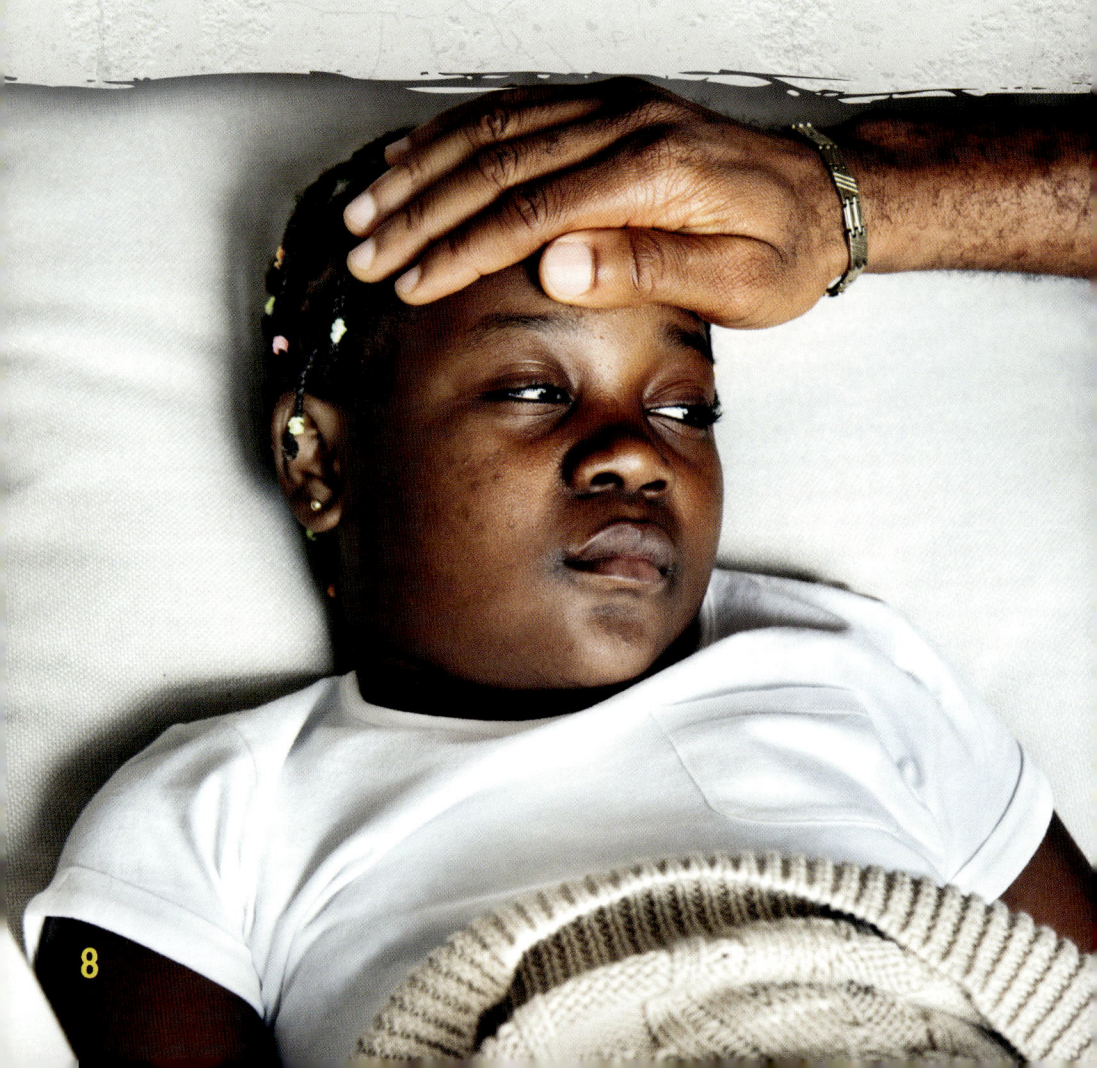

# EBOLA
## INFECTION AND SYMPTOMS

- COUGH
- RED EYES
- VOMIT
- FEVER
- RASH
- ACHES
- DIARRHEA

Patients also experience rashes, red eyes, and bleeding from **orifices**.

# SOURCE

10

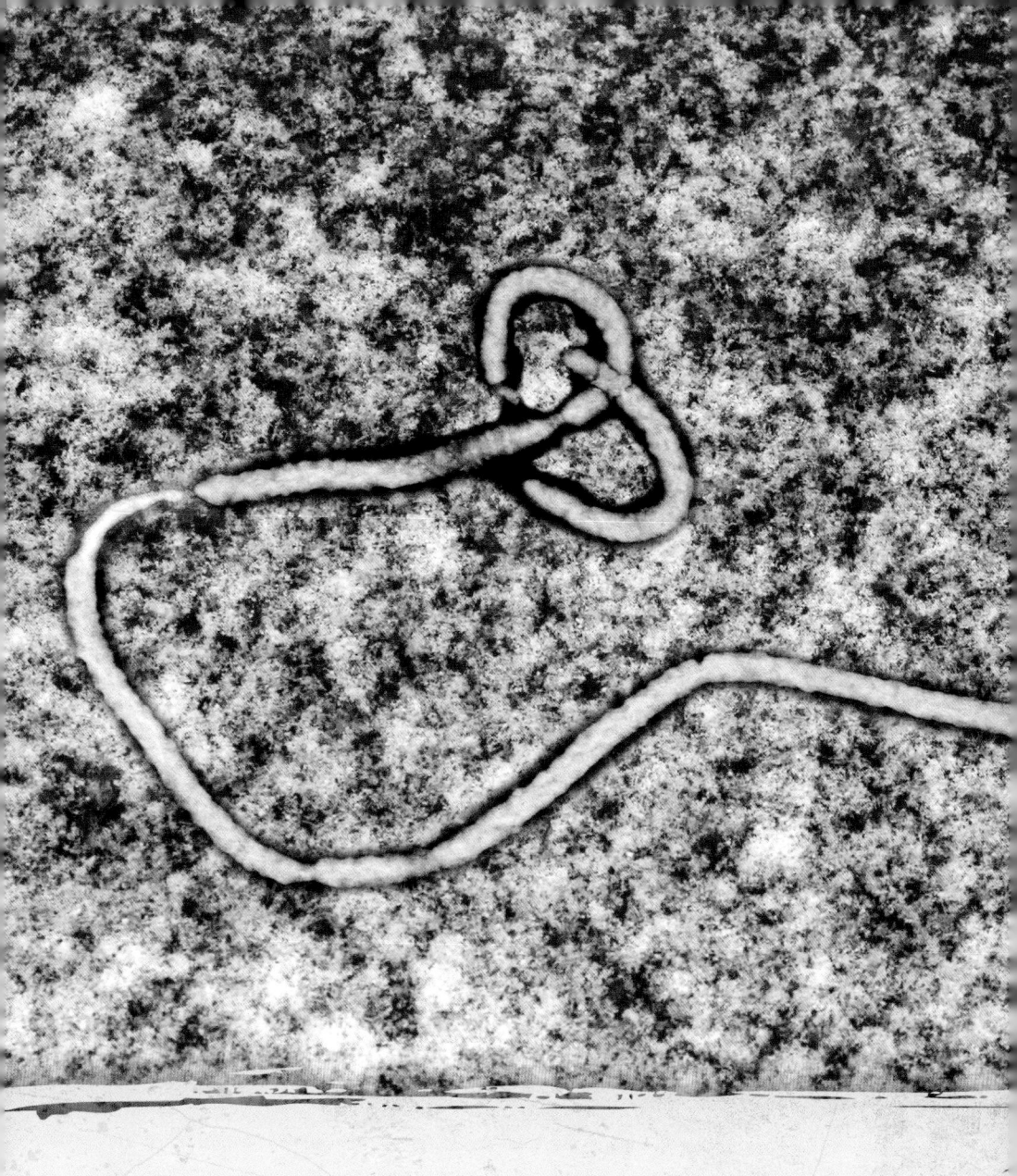

African fruit bats are thought to have spread Ebola to humans. The **infected** animals carrying the virus can **transmit** it to other animals and humans through bites or being eaten.

12

Ebola spreads from person to person through contact with bodily fluids of an **infected** person. This includes blood, saliva, and sweat.

# OUTBREAK!

**AFRICA**

Map labels: Guinea, Sierra Leone, Liberia, Gabon, Republic of the Congo, Democratic Republic of the Congo, Sudan, Uganda

■ Ebola

Ebola was first discovered in 1976 near the Ebola River in the Democratic Republic of the Congo. A storekeeper mysteriously became ill. He died five days later.

Those close to the storekeeper also became sick and died. The World Health Organization (WHO) helped stop the spread. **Isolation** kept it from becoming an **epidemic**.

The 2014-16 Ebola outbreak began in Guinea. It quickly became an **epidemic**. There were more than 28,000 cases. More than 11,000 people died.

The first case of Ebola came into the United States in 2014. An ill man arrived in Texas from West Africa. He soon died. His nurses also tested positive for Ebola.

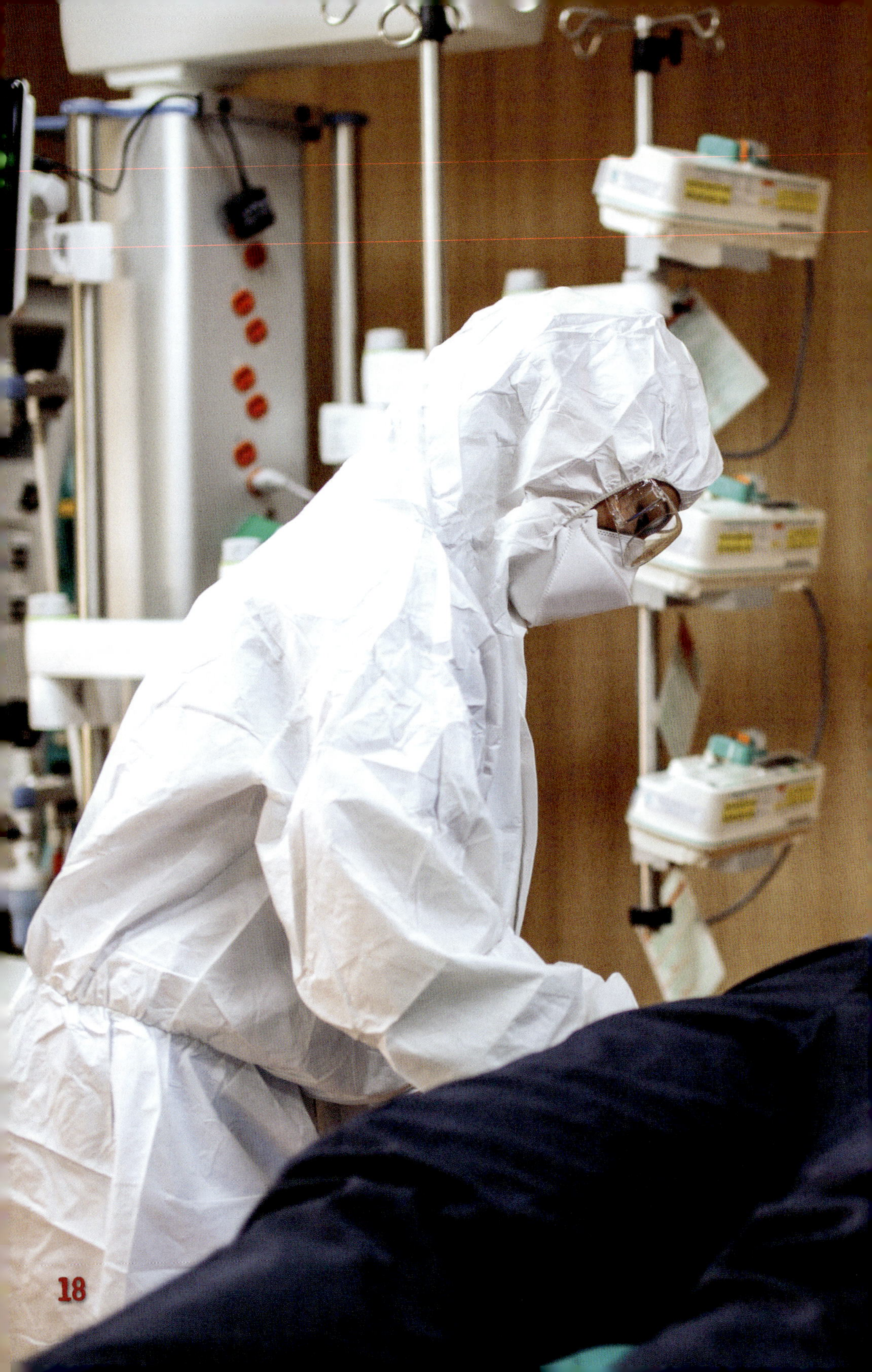

The nurses were placed in **isolation**. They were given experimental treatments. The nurses tested negative later that month.

Because of that outbreak, new **screening** methods were created at airports. Improved protective gear worn by those treating Ebola-**infected** patients were also issued.

20

In 2019, an Ebola **vaccine** was created in the US. The FDA approved it that year. It still ravages parts of Africa to this day, but there is hope with the new vaccine.

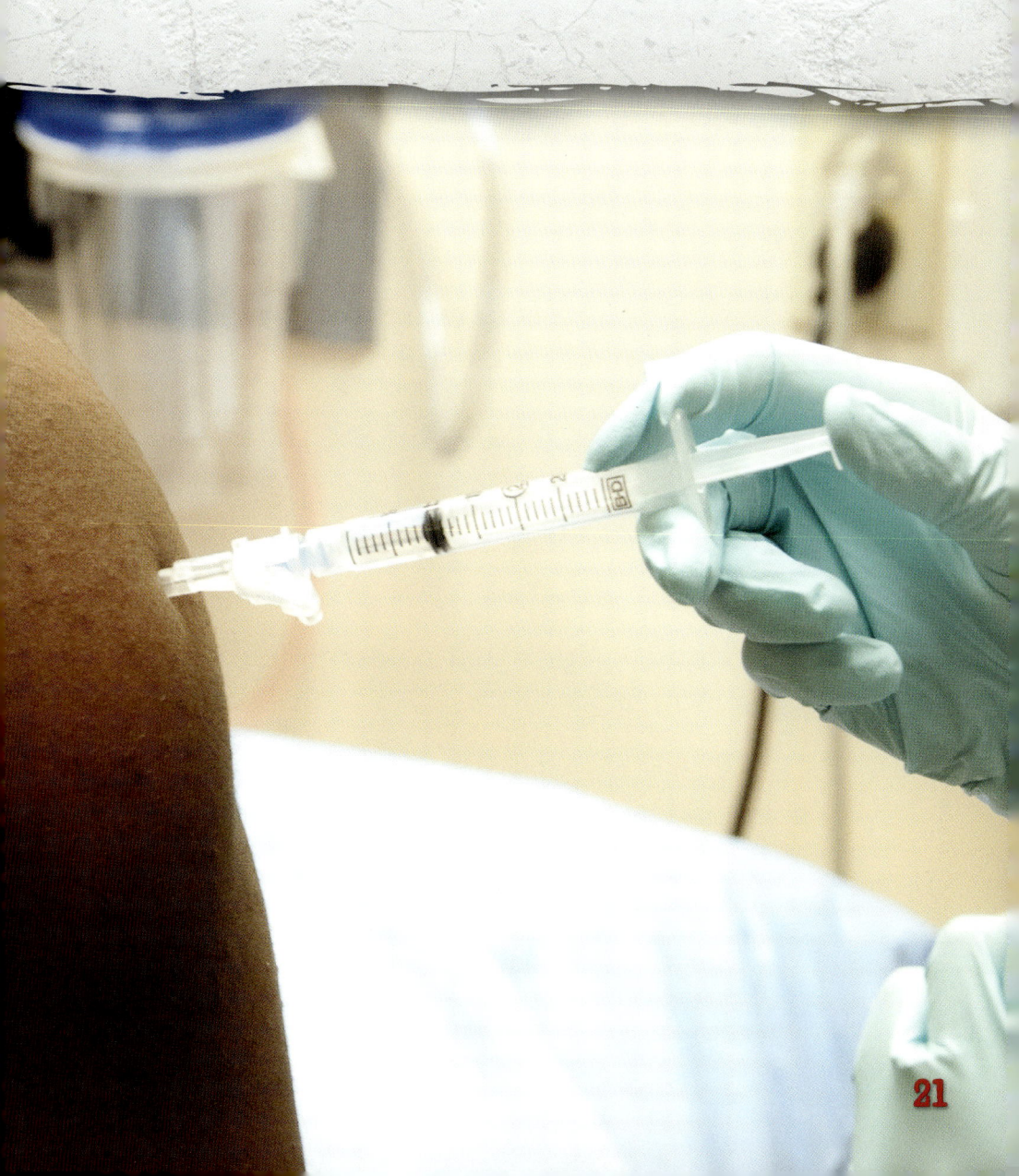

# GLOSSARY

**drylands** – an area of land that has little to no water.

**epidemic** – a disease that spreads quickly to a lot of people in a short amount of time.

**infected** – affected with a disease-causing organism.

**isolation** – to be separated from others to stop the spread of disease.

**orifice** – an opening in the body, like a nostril or mouth.

**screening** – to look for conditions that would show illness.

**symptoms** – signs that a person is ill or is becoming sick.

**transmit** – the passing of a disease to someone or something else.

**vaccine** – a medicine or cure to help end or manage an illness within someone.

# ONLINE RESOURCES

**Booklinks NONFICTION NETWORK**
FREE! ONLINE NONFICTION RESOURCES

To learn more about Ebola, please visit **abdobooklinks.com** or scan this QR code. These links are routinely monitored and updated to provide the most current information available.

# INDEX

Africa 5, 7, 11, 14, 16, 17, 21

Food and Drug Administration (FDA) 21

fruit bats 11

signs 8, 9

spread 13, 16, 17

treatments 19, 20, 21

United States 17, 21

World Health Organization (WHO) 15